Prayers for the Later Years

Prayers for the Later Years

Josephine Robertson

Abingdon Press
Nashville   New York

Introduction

At each successive stage of our lives we have special concerns. As young people we look for direction in finding our vocations and loving companions. This is followed by the busy, intense years of making a living and raising a family. When the children leave home we enter a quieter period, with fewer pressures, less financial strain, and often a need for reorientation to offset loneliness. By the time we pass the sixty-year mark, our children are adults, with their own families, and there is not very much we can do about or for them. The future no longer stretches ahead indefinitely, full of great possibilities. Now is the time we face the challenge of making a good thing of what there is.

In a collection such as this, it would be easy to catalog the obvious woes—declining health, bereavement, curtailment of activity—and I have tried to give these due attention. But I have tried, as well, to make this a book that reflects joy—stressing gratitude for past experiences, pleasure in everyday surroundings, thanks for benefits unique in modern life, prayers for perception to see the good and the beautiful around us. While not every prayer is pertinent to every reader, I hope that the book may help with perspective and in finding uncommon joy in common things.

Contents

Thanks for
Our Indian Summer

Our Father, I thank thee that we live in a time when the aged are no longer confined to chimney corners, but, in growing numbers, enjoy a mellow Indian summer. I thank thee for the medical advances which make it possible for many to enjoy latter years of learning, travel, and constructive work for church and community. I thank thee for the pensions and other provisions which help to free parents from automatic dependence on their children. Knowing, however, that there is still much misery among the neglected and forgotten, I pray that we, who are fortunate, may work for the dignity and comfort of all our aged. May we appreciate our own blessings and value the opportunities of the golden fall days which are ours. Amen.

To Live Creatively

Our Father, we thank thee that it is within our power to live creatively, even if we cannot attempt or accomplish the projects of earlier years. We think back to the pioneer grandmothers who took scraps from old coats and dresses, cut neat patches, worked out a design, and pieced quilts so beautiful that we treasure them today. Help us to take what materials we have to create a beautiful fabric of living. In the name of One whose life was supremely creative. Amen.

For the Bright
Moments of the Day

As the day ends, I thank thee for its bright moments. Remembering another morning when a brilliant hummingbird played in the stream from my watering can, I think back on the glimpses of loveliness in this day. Fleeting glimpses, easily forgotten, but I remember the smile of the little boy in the market, the unexpected loving letter, the sweet smell of earth after the shower, the laughter shared with a friend. Make me perceptive of all that is warm and beautiful, so sensing thy pervading spirit in the everyday things of life. Amen.

Thanks for Perspective

I thank thee for the perspective which one gains by climbing the mountain trail of years. From the heights I look back and see that some things I thought were disasters have worked out for the best. Troubles, which seemed insoluble in the lower forest tangles of the trail, have found solutions, and here, above timberline, I can see better what things are important. I thank thee for the experiences along the way, the good memories, the wisdom gained with pain, and the faith that for tragedies we cannot understand, there *is* a reason. Help me to keep the vision that looks beyond the immediate. Amen.

To Accept with Grace

Father, help me to learn to accept with grace the generosity of others. It is a strange feeling for one who has loved to give flowers, now to receive them from other gardens; for one who has given rides, to be a passenger. It is difficult for one who has loved independence to depend on others for help and plans. Make me, I pray, see this as an opportunity to live in the spirit of love and to show appreciation in such fashion that others may know, as I did, true joy in their giving. Amen.

For One Who Is Ill

I pray thy compassion for
one who is very ill. May he be strengthened by
the knowledge that those who care are pray-
ing for him. May he be comforted by a sense of
thy presence. If it be thy will, restore him to
health. Give strength and perception to those
who nurse him and grant him, we pray,
freedom from pain and peace of mind. In the
name of Christ who cared for the suffering.
Amen.

To Put Away Things That Are Done

Help me to live in the present rather than the past. As I put away school diplomas, my wedding dress, christening gowns, and family pictures, help me to make meaningful today's portion of my life without grieving for what is past. I stand enriched by all the experiences symbolized by these keepsakes and thank thee for them. I pray that this enrichment may make me more understanding and more responsive to the needs of others. Amen.

Prayer for
a Long Night

Help me this night, I pray, when I feel like a child lost in a forest with unknown dangers lurking in the dark shadows. Worries well up and fears take hold of me. May I have the comfort of thy hand, as that of a protecting father, to lead me through these hours until the light comes. May I rest, confident of thy care, and arise in the morning refreshed and competent to face my problems, knowing that with thee all things are possible. Amen.

To Admire

Our Father, help me, I pray, to admire what is fine in other people and to make my admiration known. I remember, when I was a child, the sudden joy when I received a pat on the head from my father, or a word of praise from my teacher. Keep me aware that human hearts are ever hungry for encouragement. I know that even people who seem so confident, the nurse who is kind, the Congressman seeking solutions, the pastor who speaks the helpful word, the editor who writes with courage, can be strengthened in their work. Help me to assure them that their efforts have impact on others. May I develop the art of searching out kindness, generosity, and courage, and then, by word or letter, show my admiration. Amen.

To Reach Out in Conversation

Help me, Father, in conversation, to draw out the thoughts of others rather than obliging them to listen to me. As Christ fathomed the deepest concerns of the woman at the well, so, in humbler fashion, may I concentrate on the things that matter to others. Keep me from laments, complaints, and monologues. Guide me in asking questions that show true interest. Help me to speak so that those with whom I speak each day may go away cheered and encouraged. Amen.

Thanks for Laughter

I thank thee that man, unlike the other creatures of earth, has capacity for laughter. Those who continue to laugh through the years have faces alight with quick perception. I thank thee that when we laugh together it creates a bond like a rainbow, bringing us close regardless of age, and it is a healing thing. Help us to smile, to cultivate the habit of kindly enjoyment of the gambols of kittens, the droll word, the odd happening, the entertainer who works to please us, and not least, the jokes upon ourselves. Since even in ancient times it was known that "a merry heart doeth good like medicine," help us to make joy a way of life, knowing that it warms the hearts of others and so is a way of worship. Amen.

Thanks for Faith

I thank thee that in a country church, with clean light streaming across the pew, with the song of birds joining the choir through the open windows, I was suddenly aware of how much faith can mean. I thank thee that not only in the churches built by men, but in any situation, one may turn to thee in the sanctuary of one's heart. May we, in our later years, treasure this privilege and still catch the song of the birds through the open windows of our spirits. Amen.

On Leaving a Longtime Home

Our Father, it is not easy to leave a home where there has been so much love and so much living, to start a different way of life. As I part with the things I will no longer be using—the chairs, dishes, rugs, tables—I feel as though part of me goes with each item, so deeply entwined are they with family memories. Help me to realize that these are only physical things and that the love they symbolize will go with me. May I face forward cheerfully, resolved to concentrate on all the good aspects of my new situation. Be with me and help me, I pray. Amen.

To Overcome Loneliness

Dear God, sometimes I feel like an empty shell cast up and left on the beach by the outgoing tide. Help me to face my loneliness, realizing that it is not mine alone, but a condition common to many whose dear ones are beyond the reach of human voices and whose strength no longer permits many of the things they would like to do. Help me, this day, to reach out to someone else who is unhappy, to plan something to anticipate, to offer my services where they are needed, or to make something—for there is joy in creation, even if it is an apron or a birdhouse. Help me, I pray, to dispel my emptiness with cheerful purpose. Amen.

Thanks for the New Day

Our Father, I thank thee for this morning, for the rising sun that paints the windows gold, for the blue sky with pink-tinged clouds. May I always keep my wonder at the beauty of thy world, even when I can only see it in glimpses. Keep my spirit as fresh as this young day. Remembering how Christ walked through the fields, sensitive to their beauty, and yet turning it to use in his teachings, so may I move through this new day, living with purpose and with love. Amen.

For Relating to
the Young

I pray for the gift of understanding, that I may communicate with the young people who are striking out to cut new trails through the tangle of today's problems. It is easy to condemn their ways because their code is not the code so forcibly impressed on us in our youth. Help me to realize that, as their dilemmas and pressures are different, so their reactions and answers are different. I thank thee that they care enough to seek a fulfilling way of life. Help me not to judge, but to reach out in love to hurt and hungry hearts. Amen.

Prayer for an Alienated Youth

God, who loves all thy children, I pray for the aimless, dirty youth, who has chosen squalor to cleanliness, apathy to vigor, drifting to purpose. While, reluctantly, we admire his rejection of physical comforts, his indifference to material things, and his willingness to share what he has, it hurts us who are older to see him apparently squandering his youth, his health, his opportunities for constructive work. Save him from the self-destruction of drugs, and as he matures, may he see that society needs him. Help him to realize his potential and, with understanding gleaned from these cast-off years, help him, I pray, to find fulfillment and to serve his fellowmen. Amen.

After Stepping Down

Our Father, when I see someone else doing the work, holding the offices, and receiving the attention I did, help me to praise and give support. Keep me from stressing "the way *we* did" or announcing "*we* tried that and it didn't work." If my experience can be useful, help me to share it—when someone asks. In time of difficulty, may I speak the right words of encouragement. As the child playing games learns that he cannot be *it* all the time, so help me to participate unobtrusively and cheerfully. Amen.

For One Who Is Confused

I ask thy compassion on one who is groping, like a traveler, through a thick fog of confusion. Remembering the quick spirit, the purposeful activity of this person in former years, we who love him come to thee in sorrow. May those who take care of him have patience, gentleness, and perception. If it be thy will, restore him to the recognition of people and life around him. If this is not to be, grant that his spirit may be untroubled and that his dreams may be sweet. With our love we commend this dear soul to thee. Amen.

For One Who Is Depressed

I pray for one who is living under a lowering cloud that cuts off the rays of the sun. He sees only frustration and emptiness ahead. The fire of his spirit has gone out, leaving only ashes. I pray that, through thy inspiration, one who cares may find the way to fan some ember that still remains. Through the skilled help of friend, doctor, or pastor, may he be restored, finding use for his talents and enjoyment in fellowship with others. I pray for him in the name of Christ, who led men into the meaningful path of life. Amen.

For a Retiree

Our Father, be with the man who has emptied his desk, turned in his last report, laid down his tools, and closed his office door. Help him not to be regretful when he sees his purposeful neighbor striding off to work and, when he encounters a former colleague, finds that the work is going along perfectly well without him. Keep him from apathy and help him to see this change not as an end, but as the beginning of new opportunities to enjoy, to learn, to serve in ways for which he has never had time. Grant that these years may be fruitful and full of zest. Amen.

For a Retiree's Wife

Help her to remember, I pray, that she married her husband because her greatest desire was to be with him. Through the years his path has led away from home into the world of affairs. Hers has made a circle from her own work, home, through the neighborhood, church, shopping center, and organizations. Help her now to change her pattern graciously, if need be, to recover the old companionship. Grant her the patience and love to rebuild confidence in her husband when he feels like a displaced person. May they find projects to enjoy together and individually. I pray that these years, close together, may be rich in love and service. Amen.

When Feeling Neglected

Help me to rise above the ache that comes when one feels forgotten. Busy people cannot understand how much a letter, a phone call, or a visit means, or how great, in our later years, is the hunger for reassurance and affection. Forgive me for my own heedlessness in the past. Instead of brooding with self-pity, help me to reach out to surprise and lift another's spirit. Help me to make allowances, to love generously, remembering that love "seeketh not her own" —and is kind. So may I be. Amen.

In Time of Loss
of One Greatly Loved

Give me the courage, I pray, to face the loss of one I have loved so deeply. Looking back through the years when our lives were so close, it seems that part of me has died as well. Help me not to be bitter, but to dwell on the privilege of our intimacy and to thank thee for a good life, well and generously lived. Although we can no longer speak, may the inspiration remain with me. I thank thee for the comfort of knowing that the bright spirit of one I have loved is with thee. Amen.

For Serenity in
Facing Weakness

I thank thee for the example of men and women I have known, who have accepted physical limitations with sweetness, and particularly one frail person of whom it was said that her presence was like a benediction. For one who has been strong it is hard to accept weakness, knowing that physical vitality will not return. Grant that I may have radiance of spirit, concerned always with others rather than myself. I am grateful for the bright days of summer I have enjoyed, as now, in the autumn of my life, the grass turns brown and the russet leaves of the trees drift down. I thank thee that, unlike the psalmist who saw this as a symbol of empty death, Christ taught that our essential spirit is immortal. Amen.

Thanks for Prayer

I thank thee for the privilege of prayer. As the glider pilot, without power of his own, learns to soar on invisible winds and updrafts, so we, with faith, find uplifting power to carry us above the fears and problems that surround us. I thank thee, too, that we may bring thee our concerns for others. Though we may be far apart and unable to help, we have the comfort of committing them to thy care. As the pilot sees earth from great heights, so may we, through prayer, view our own and our friends' concerns with fresh perspective and return to our daily lives inspired and refreshed. Amen.

Thanks for Friends

I thank thee for the gift of friendship and shared enjoyment, refreshing as a spring rain that makes the leaves sparkle and the fragrance of damp roses sweet on the air. I thank thee that as I know the talents and weaknesses of my friends, so they, in thine own spirit, accept me with all my faults. In times of unhappiness, I am grateful for the comfort they bring. May I, in turn, share deeply in both joy and sorrow. Give me the skill to turn complaint and bitterness to more helpful thoughts. I thank thee for the dear companions now gone, for my young friends with sparkling eyes and spirits, and for those who are contemporaries, who share past experiences—and who understand. Amen.

To Marvel

Help me, I pray, to retain the fresh interest of the child who finds a starfish on the beach, a blue robin's egg, a shiny acorn fitting perfectly in its little cup. May I marvel at the shape of snowflakes, the structure of a columbine, the pattern of feathers on a hummingbird. May I care enough to learn the names of the flowers along the roadside, the trees in the park, the birds that jostle each other at the feeder, the stars that shine above us. "When I consider thy heavens . . . ," wrote the psalmist, "the moon and stars, which thou hast ordained; what is man, that thou art mindful of him?" But we know that, beyond the beauty of this world, thou *art* mindful of us, and we thank thee. Amen.

To Be a Contributing Member

Our Father, in all my activities, help me to contribute in some constructive fashion. When I assume responsibilities, may I be dependable. If I agree to do some job, may I do it, not grudgingly, but with joy. When I have suggestions, may they be helpful and given quietly. When I am a member of an audience, may the speaker or artist find in my face attention and response, emphasized later by words of appreciation. When financial support is needed, may I give what I have wisely where it will help the most. In working with others, give me enthusiasm and help me, I pray, always to be a contributing member of society. Amen.

To Face the
Inevitable

Our Father, as I look back across my life with all its changing scenes, it seems like a tale in a book, but I do not know the end. Perhaps it is well that, unlike impatient children, we cannot look ahead to see how the story comes out. But so many pages have been turned that I know the end of the book is near. Help me to face the inevitable without fear or dismay. Grant me the power to live fully all my days, aware of the wonders of life, accepting what limitations I must, not agonizing over the *why's* of what happens, but strong in the *how's* of my response. In the spirit of Christ, I pray. Amen.

Upon Retirement

Help me, I pray, as I face this new, uncharted way of life. I feel adrift, knowing that I am no longer essential to the enterprise which gave my life purpose, gave my family security, and gave me the comradeship of fellow workers. I welcome the freedom from responsibility, a long vacation—but is this enough? Guide me, I pray, into useful activity, less demanding than my former work, but putting such skills as I have to use in a new way. In the past I have been in command. Teach me now to serve. Amen.

Thanks for
New Horizons

I thank thee for the fellowship of those whom I know through books, whose ideas open up new vistas of thought, whose adventures take me into the world of action. I thank thee that "walls do not a prison make" because of the companionship of men and women who reach out to me through the printed word, the recorded word and song, and the near-human presence of television. I thank thee that no longer, as in early times, man's knowledge of things beyond sight must come from the tales of a wandering bard, but that today we transcend time and space to meet the great of past and present in our own homes. Help me gratefully to make use of these opportunities to broaden my understanding all the days of my life. Amen.

To Think Modern

Our Father, today I watched an old giant of a tree in the midst of savage winds—its branches tossed, its leaves scattering, but riding out the storm because its roots go deep. Even so in our world, new ideologies, new patterns of behavior, threaten the stability we have known. Like a devastating storm, these attacking winds can level forests where the roots are shallow. Give me an open mind, I pray. Keep me receptive to new ideas, but I pray that my roots in faith and in the power of Christ's goodness may go ever deeper and be my strength. Amen.

To Treasure
the Ballot

Our Father, I thank thee that I live in a country where I may cast my vote with privacy and freedom. I thank thee that my vote counts just as much as those of younger, influential men. Help me to use it wisely, taking time to study the issues, talk with those around me, and read the articles, not just the headlines, about important matters that may look dull compared to the sports or entertainment pages. In a world where individual freedom is threatened, help me to treasure my privileges as a citizen and to work toward strengthening this freedom in those parts of our country where, shamefully, it is abrogated. Help me, I pray, to know, to care, and to act. Amen.

To Change
the Focus

Our Father, as years advance and I cannot do the things I once did, help me to change the focus, as I do with my camera, from sweeping panoramas to the beauty of things seen close. Help me to enjoy the flowers on the windowsill as I loved a garden; the birds at the feeder as the birds I used to walk to see on country roads; the play on television, when theater was once a joy; the cup of coffee with a friend instead of a party; my small, cozy rooms instead of the old house. Help me to realize that enjoyment resides not in things, but in my attitude toward them. Grant, I pray, the power to find uncommon joy in common things. Amen.

On Making a Will

Give me the wisdom, I pray, to channel what I have in thoughtful ways. These possessions and this money which I call mine are only mine for a time and will, before long, go to others. Help me to be generous— wisely. I think of the words we have sung so many times, "All things come of thee, O Lord, and of thine own have we given thee," as I designate a portion for thy work—as though putting it, with gratitude, into a great collection plate. May my bequests to individuals be helpful, contributing to their happiness. Humbly I pray, too, that I may leave them more than property, as the legacies of love and character from those who have gone before mean so much to me. I thank thee for whatever I have to give. Amen.

For Our Country

I thank thee for the privilege of living in a beautiful, new country, close enough to pioneer days to remember some who risked everything to turn wilderness into farms and communities. Help this country, with all its resources, to be a shining light in the world. Forgive us and guide us in atoning for injustices to our blacks, Indians, Spanish-Americans, and Orientals. Lead us into the paths of peace, not war, that the killing of men and women and little children may cease to be the terrible yet accepted pattern of settling differences. Grant wisdom and integrity to our leaders—and wisdom to us as we choose them. Make us, as citizens, watchful, so that from the grassroots, word may go to our officials that Americans want a land of opportunity, justice, and goodwill. Amen.

To Make Our World Clean

As the housewife realizes that the time has come for a great housecleaning, so thy people know today that the time has come to sweep clean the beautiful world thou hast given us. Help us to make our rivers and lakes and skies fresh again and our hillsides uneroded. We pray for the day when our stores of terrible gases and destructive chemicals may be eliminated without harm. May each of us care enough to take action, sacrificial if need be, in order that we may see our mountains again, unsoiled by dingy clouds, our waterfronts sparkling, and our beaches safe for our children's children. We pray, with the psalmist, that once again "the heavens rejoice and earth be glad." Amen.

To Remember the Concerns of Others

Help me, I pray, to be mindful of the times which have special meaning for others: birthdays, anniversaries, dates on which things happened that were sad or happy. In the years when families are no longer close-knit, supportive circles, and when old friends are especially precious, help me to enter into the joys and griefs of those around me. As the candles on a cake glow with meaning, not just to mark the years, but to show the love of one who cared enough to put them there, so may I light candles of remembrance to warm the hearts of my friends. Amen.

To Bridge the Years with Interests

I thank thee for the many interests that can reach across the gulf of years to establish live contact between the minds and hands of different generations. Age is forgotten when a white-haired man builds a model ship with his little grandson, when a grandmother paints with younger friends, or when singers of many ages create harmony in a choir. Help me to keep my interests alive, such skills as I have, polished, that I may have something to share, perhaps to contribute, to others. I thank thee for the pleasure and refreshment to be found in younger friends. Amen.

To Live in Love

Help me to understand in depth the importance of loving one another, for then, as John writes, we dwell in God and he in us, for he is love. When my reaction is to dislike or hate, help me to understand. When I feel resentment, hurt pride, or slight, help me to see how demeaning is this response. As a loving mother loves no less, but tries to fathom the cause of her child's behavior, so may I care about those who are difficult—and try to help. Remembering how a shaft of sunlight can transfigure a lowering day, may I ever seek the love that has transforming radiance. Amen.

Thanks for a
Close-Knit World

Our Father, I thank thee that I live in an age unlike that of my great-grandparents, who waved good-bye to sons sailing off to a new world and never saw them again. I am grateful for the inventions accepted as commonplace today—planes that carry people and letters swiftly, recordings of voices bringing loving messages, snapshots of beloved babies showing just how they look, telephones that can make voices from Australia sound like those from around the corner. We know how profoundly true it is that "as cold waters to a thirsty soul, so is good news from a far country," and we pray that in using our new means of communication we may convey messages of good news, love, encouragement, and appreciation. Amen.

For a Young Pastor
(or Doctor)

How strange it seems that the pastor, a person whom, for many years, I looked up to as a father figure, is young enough to be my son—or grandson—and that he, who has had so much less experience in living than I, should be concerned with my well-being. Bless him in his work, grant him special understanding and wisdom. I know that his path is not easy, for it demands personal sacrifice and courage in the face of criticism. I thank thee that in an age of doubt and cynicism there are young men dedicating their lives to service, and I pray that in ways unforeseen, I may be of help to him. Amen.

Upon a Class Reunion

Our Father, we are aware of the years abruptly when we see the men who have always stayed handsome in our memories now bald and heavy; the graceful, golden-haired girls now wrinkled and worn almost beyond recognition. And I know I look as strange to them. Yet, I am the same person inside. I thank thee that the strangeness wears off and we find the basic characters unchanged—the people we once worked with, played with, and loved, still there. I thank thee for this renewed spark of touching minds and hearts. Help me always to look beyond the exterior to the essential spirit within. In the name of One who changes not. Amen.

For a New Grandchild

Bless, I pray, this beautiful child, so newly come into our family. I thank thee for the wonder and privilege of looking, for the first time, on the tiny face of our child's child. We anticipate his first smiles, first words, first steps, and pray that he may flourish in a climate of affection. May we be a loving link for him with an earlier generation. I pray that he may grow up into a peaceful world where he may realize all his potential, maturing from a happy childhood to a life of accomplishment and service. Amen.

For Compassion
in Retrospect

Our Father, as I look through a box of yellowed family photographs, my parents and others, who once seemed so old to me, now look so young—younger than I. Their faces fresh, unlined, innocent, appear to look to me and ask for understanding. I now know more about their problems than I could in my youth. Forgive me for the past blindness and impatience which must have caused them pain. I thank thee for their love and that in their youth and inexperience they did their best for their children. May I always think of them and the other members of our families with love. For those who were difficult, whose actions caused resentment and friction, grant me loving understanding. Wipe old grudges from my heart, I pray, and replace them with compassion. Amen.

To Listen

Help me, I pray, to listen, aware that this is a simple service, but that there are few willing listeners and there are many people longing for a sympathetic ear. Make me patient with repetition, interested in people and events long gone, and skillful in turning, with a quiet word, thoughts to brighter channels and present concerns. Just as children come home bursting with news, eager for someone to tell, so there are older ones longing for the chance to unburden their thoughts to one who cares. Make me, I pray, an unhurried, creative listener, humbly following in the path of One who listens to all men. Amen.

Thanks for Those Who Care

I thank thee for those who have chosen vocations of serving the elderly in a society where so many persons are no longer members of family units. I thank thee that with kindness, warmth, and understanding, these dedicated men and women reach out to those who are not their kin. Bless them in their work, grant them wisdom to bring comfort and meaning to the lonely and helpless. May they know the reward of appreciation and the knowledge that as they serve, they are serving thee. Amen.

For Courage Not to Give Up

Keep me, I pray, from the devastating feeling of "what's the use?" When the days ahead look hopeless, with friends gone, uncertain health, and little to anticipate, teach me still to treasure life. May I live as best I can, with concern for others, with deliberate effort to learn, to care, to smile, to reach out, to live fully each day, not dreading tomorrow. May I have faith, in the words of the ancient psalm, that "thou wilt light my candle; the Lord my God will enlighten my darkness." Amen.

On a Thin
Wedding Band

I thank thee, Father, for the meaning of this timeworn wedding ring, blessed in a sacrament many years ago. It was shiny then, even as our faces were young, unlined, glowing with hope for the future. Through this bond we have known joy and sorrow, struggle and achievement, children, a busy home—gradually grown quiet—and the delight of grandchildren. We have experienced the richness of family life and the joy of companionship. I thank thee that our marriage vows have meant so much and for the fulfillment symbolized by this thin gold band. Amen.

For Something That Is Lost Forever

Our Father, it is hard to face the loss of something that has meant so much in my life and has brought so much joy. It would be easy to let this loss darken my whole outlook. Help me to realize how much is left. I remember a plane takeoff under a near-black sky—a struggle upward through the clouds and sudden emergence into sunshine and blue skies for the rest of the journey. Help me to struggle through this cloud, confident of brightness ahead. Amen.

To Comfort

Speak through me, I pray, at those times when I try to comfort one who is suffering physical pain or loss. Help me to know when to speak, when to listen, and when a hand on another's arm means more than words. As Jesus wept for his friends' sorrow, teach me to share and not to minimize another's despair; and teach me, too, how to offer my assurance and support for the road ahead. In thy spirit may I stand with and help a troubled soul. Amen.